The Cycles of Creation

A New Testament of Life
Cycle II: Aquarius

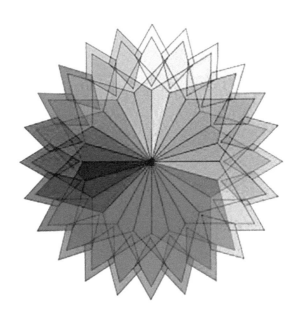

Clif LaPlant

NEWMAN SPRINGS PUBLISHING
320 Broad Street
Red Bank, NJ 07701

First originally published by Newman Springs Publishing 2024

ISBN 979-8-89308-098-8 (Paperback)
ISBN 979-8-89308-099-5 (Digital)

Printed in the United States of America

The "Laniakea Supercluster," Hawaiian for "Open Skies" or "Immense Heaven" is the home of the "Milky Way" galaxy of our World along with all of its Ancient Indigenous Civilizations.

To Lahaina…

Contents

Star of Faith

Stars of Creation

These energy stars each bring forth frequencies of light encodement from creation for all on our journey of self-empowerment, soul growth, and illumination. Each of us is an individual expression of the living light on our journey of light expansion in form from our core soul level of creation.

We each have our own energy prism of light, just as each snowflake does, which is unique for everyone. This beautiful revelation and reality of life has been proven by the images of frozen water molecules taken by Masaru Emoto under different energy applications.

I invite everyone to use these Stars of Creation on your journey of expansion. To meditate with, and also bathe in their radiance. Color and sound are the essence of light that is the foundation of our physical reality.

I invite you all to visit the Stars of Creation with Clif LaPlant and Brian Foster Porter at *starsofcreation.com* and our Instagram *@thestarsofcreation*.

PS. Meditating and spending time with the stars—in particular, the one in association with each chapter—before and after reading, will help expand the energy experience for all.

May the Stars Be with You!
starsofcreation.com

Preface

This book has been written in an energetic and synergistic fashion of outline, to relay for all an energy association and doorway for our mind and heart to enter together in a new energy alliance. The repetitive outlines and associations are for ease of a clear perspective and understanding of very important information; but they are also, in reality, an energetic frequency release for past profile conditioning. This is to assist all to move forward now, as all our realities begin to change. I wish all to try to keep an open mind and have faith in themselves with creation. We all are our Creator's children and will eventually become our great god self within, with our Creator's love, light, and perfection guiding each of us on our journey of life, our journey of light.

I put forth now that I refer to our Creator as a representation of the head of all the religions. My personal feeling is that there is only one Creator and all humanity is experiencing a spiritual existence from the same source.

With love, light, and respect for all of creation
Clifford Kenneth Platt III
a.k.a Clif LaPlant

Prologue

Here we all are; round 2, book 2. With me at the helm of my book-ships sailing them into the future, our future. I am a passenger too on this vessel, Planet Earth, sailing forth into a brand-new level of light, reality, and life on and with her.

The essence of reality of the way the world has really been, the real in reality of our past creations here on Planet Earth are mind-boggling, unbelievable at best. The seven wonders of the world, megalithic human skeletons, lost civilizations resurfacing, ancient landmark creations that we do not have the technology to recreate.

What I am sharing here is the opportunity for everyone reading this material to realize that all these past civilizations and life-forms that were created were real and did exist. These energies of creation are still here, they still exist along the timeline of creation.

Now our Creator's hand is coming forth once again to temper and guide humanity forth on its new path of learning. To help us all see both sides of the coin, so to speak. So we may all understand why the righteous path is the right one and find our way to it, get on it, and stay on it. This is a very personal inside process for all. Our devices will not assist us at this level. Maybe science will create a spiritual GPS.

The four elements of creative form are all surging forth once again. The cosmos is realigning for this next level of light. All creation throughout time and space is coming into a oneness of frequency now.

Book 1, *The Presence* was written to open the door and present to all the ability to see, feel, and open on a basic energy level to the changes that creation is bringing forward now for us all.

Book 2, *Aquarius* is about how this shift of our new realities of life will take place. It is an outline of what each soul will go through on this next journey of light. Its basic energy format is about acceptance. For each soul to move forward, we each must go within to open our heart to our soul's true essence, and that begins with surrender, acceptance, and faith.

This is huge! In itself, just aligning ourselves to begin this process, let alone going through it and living it. But that is what we all must do now. The time is now for all who wish to move forward onto their highest energetic profile of light. Once again, I relate to each reader that this information is an energetic profile and beginning for each to find their own way. To unlock each individual aspect of our Creator according to their vibrational and energetic encodement of love and light. Just as each of the droplets of water together makes an ocean, they also each spend time as a snowflake.

We are all on our journey of creation…

So now stop and look at this world. What I see and feel now everywhere, for the most part, is fear and chaos. This is because there is so much imbalance in our world. Now this imbalance is becoming very visible because of the light coming to Mother Earth and to each of us. The love of creation is coming to clean up its home and plant a new garden for a new season of growth.

During this new season and cycle of growth, creation will apply all the learning that was amassed from this last growth period at a higher vibratory rate.

We as a race of light beings of form, and also our light-body planet, are growing and evolving always. Creation has planted its seed in each and every one of us. We are the garden. In this next cycle, we will all live much closer to and with our planet in many new ways. We will all have a much deeper connection with source, our planet, each other, and last but not least, ourselves.

This new way of life for all will be clean, clear, bright, and alive with empowerment and fulfillment for all in every way, every day. This is all very real and very possible. Once again, I ask each of you to open your heart to feel these words. Read them slowly and precisely until you have finished. Read, reread, breathe, and feel. When you are all finished, then decide what you feel and how you think. I bring these words forth with the highest love for you all on your journey of light.

For those of you that have found that spark, that fire, of this new life that is coming forward now, there is plenty we each can do to enable and empower ourselves.

For those reading this material and having difficulty or other emotions with your process, I ask you to do your best to just read this material and then to form your opinion and feeling about how you feel as a whole about all this material.

What I am saying to you all now is that even those souls that have a problem with these words, it is because it is triggering your emotional and mental process. This alone is a catalyst for your change also. So even in not serving you, these words still do.

By opening ourselves to become more empowered with love inside and outside, on and with our physical, mental, emotional, and spiritual bodies, we build our house of light. Our new journey of light begins now.

Aquarius Welcomes You
to Infinity and Beyond!

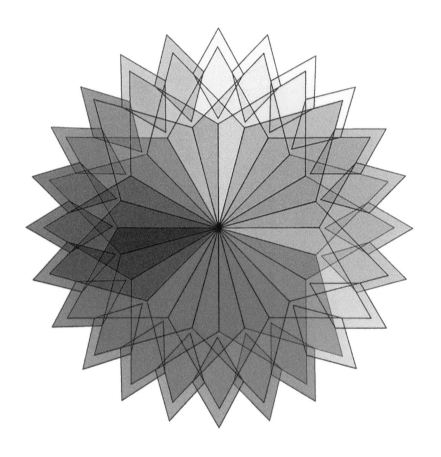

Star of Aquarius

The Aquarian Awakening

Our solar system and Planet Earth, along with all its inhabitants, are entering a new age of light and enlightenment. A bold new Age of Aquarius filled with all-new energies of creation.

Our world as we know it will never be the same again. Change, change, change, and more change of enlightenment, empowerment, embodiment, and illumination of more wisdom, love, and grace for all of humanity and creation on every level of creation.

Each and every soul provides creation with parameters of energy expressions for creation to expand its horizons of reality energetically.

Now all the conditions of light have been met for the finalization of this calendar of time and space and its rebirth.

All souls will now bear witness to this completion we each have played a role in creating, as each of our creative realities come forth to be expressed as our own individual truth and reality of life.

The real in reality of all our expressions of life will provide a common denominator for humanity to shift its focus of life to life.

We each must hold a position of love and acceptance without judgment for all our brothers and sisters on their road to salvation and envision their expression and expansion of light as it is appropriate to serve their soul and also serve creation itself.

Greatness knows no bounds or boundaries. There is a time and timing for all of creation to shine its light in the microcosm and macrocosm of our Creator's universe of living light.

This is our time now, to shine our light, in a whole new way, for those who are ready, willing, accountable, and responsible in this new, new living light of creation and new Age of Aquarius.

Aquarius Beckons Us
Always Remember, We Are

Braver than we Believe
Stronger than we Imagine
Smarter than we Think
Better than we Feel
Loved more than we Know
A part of creation Forever

Believe, Imagine, Think, Feel, Know Forever…

Global Gateway Star

Chapter 1

Completion

The energies of creation are shining their brightest yet. Regardless of previous analogy, structure, and even scripture to a great degree, all creation is now realigning itself. What has been will now all change. I talk now of the future present moment of time, space, and creation. My best advice for all is the living of the reality of the present moment.

Our creator is now redirecting all of creation to a new alignment of energetic progression of the reality of time and space. What has been will now all change to a very great degree. The expansion of this aperture of consciousness on all levels is taking place right now. The energy of this narrative will only encompass what is and what will be by completing and releasing what has been.

This completion of time and space is now taking place throughout our universe and will include all creation in existence. This redirection and realignment will now support all levels of existence from a new and higher energetic platform of reality. All reality always receives the same energetic light quotient of creation in direct relation to its energetic sphere of influence. So all reality always receives the same energies of creation relative to its energetic platform of creation. This occurs at the frequency aligned with each individual dimensional sphere of creation. The Presence of our Creator's Light expands with Creation.

The presence of the Nemesis Star System and Planet Nibiru itself are the key and culminating factor for this shift and realignment to occur. As this shift occurs, it places us all squarely in the Aquarian Age.

Our first house of redirection and realignment of this new cycle of creation comes to us all new. Many have their own individual belief of zodiac alignment, function, and progression. While many forms of astrology do not associate Aquarius as the first house or Pisces as the last house of the Zodiac of the Ages, this is exactly where we are and what is taking place. We are ending this cycle within the final stage of the house of Pisces. This cycle change, that I talk about, will occur with this finalization. Our new cycle of creation will begin in the house of Aquarius.

The energy of this house reveals to us all the premise and promise of our future reality that prophecy has foretold of. Creation is revealing itself to all in a new way with a higher level of spiritual understanding of companionship and soul essence of form. The Aquarian light frequencies coming forward now are bringing all reality into its final process of experience, learning, expansion, and embodiment energetically of this current platform of creation, aligning all creation to begin our next cycle.

The energies of creation of this current cycle timeline are now culminating and are being condensed together into a harmonic unity and oneness that represents its total energetic reality and or body of experience of creation.

This shift taking place represents individual embodiments of physical form along with their soul growth and expansion. It also represents the complete energetic profile of all creation, for each civilization, for all life-forms, for each soul's expression with creation, for Mother Earth's evolution, for our galaxy, and our universe. In other words, every aspect of this last creative cycle, right down to the last grain of sand.

Each soul here now has the opportunity to redirect and realign itself with all it has been in relation to all of this creative force right now. So with all that said, now we come to the physical plane level of light in form of physical embodiment. This means bringing this light into our physical body and walking the earth in that body of light. This is the difference in reality of this new cycle that is beginning right now.

Now as this current cycle of light is ending, humanity is being provided the opportunity to align its energies of creation and bring them into an alliance and balance of completion. This is not a mental process although the mind plays a role in this process. It is, in fact, an energy process of heart and soul. There is no right or wrong here, no good or bad, no way of figuring this out. There is only the light, love, and perfection of each present moment creating balance, harmony, and union of self.

So how does this process take place? I will tell you. It takes place with desire, truth, love, patience, and faith.

Yes, indeed, not mental nor emotional, yet they play an important role in our process of self-empowerment and self-enlightenment. So now as all these past and present energies of creation are aligning for the finalization of this cycle, we are all experiencing a multitude of emotions and thoughts presenting themselves worldwide as deep feelings that have been suppressed and compressed over time and space that are being expressed now.

Voluntary or involuntary expression is entering a critical mass energy focal point now as energy timelines condense and recoordinate themselves together into a oneness of energetic expression. All of creation is becoming what it truly is in relation to all the energy it has created.

The real in reality for all of creation and for every soul here now is revealing itself now. It cannot be held back or contained any longer. The window of creation of this last cycle is closing and revealing the essence of its creation on all levels of creation.

The energies of cause and effect from all directions of energetic progression are all now redirecting themselves into a proponent of creative mass. This is why humanity is changing so fast now. The lower kingdom of creation, which has entrenched itself so well within society and our beautiful planet, is now being brought forth into the light of day to be revealed openly.

The energetic culmination of this last cycle must be expressed now. The true form of creative mass must be expressed now for each individual. Truth will be the order of the day, and insurmountable by anyone or anything. We each are witnessing this fact every day now. Humanity is expressing itself very outwardly and openly now on all levels. People everywhere seem to have very little control over themselves and their forms of expression. This is going to increase and expand in every way.

So here, now, the energies of culmination are upon us…

These frequencies are the driving force behind all this change occurring now. All of creation has its own form of energetic projection and relativity. This means that all that is occurring has been created to occur. This also means that there are no mistakes. Especially now in this time of completion. I am sure many do not see this period this way, but that is exactly what it is.

For those of you reading this material, I put forth to you all the concept now to look at ourselves and then to look at the world. To see everything and yet judge nothing. To just breathe and feel the reality of the world without any judgment. Breathe and feel with no thought, just breathe and feel…as we relax into our moment of creation and reflect on our reality of life, especially our personal judgments. Then we begin to experience only our true feelings and our own truth.

As we begin to breathe and feel this world that is moving so fast around us, we begin to feel and know what it is that we are in relation to this world. We begin to feel the part of this reality that is ours and then begin to release the part that is not.

So now I project to you all the perfecting of this process and moving forward to now breathe and feel our truth and our reality and let all else pass us by. Letting it all just go by on its journey of creation and not make it a part of our journey of creation. Not our truth, and not our reality. To not judge and empower it and take it upon ourselves, to not wear it and own it as our reality if it is not truly a part of our reality of life.

Our projections, thoughts, words, and deeds must be our own with our own truth empowering them. I invite everyone now to be and live your own truth, whatever it is. Each drop of water, each snowflake is its own prism of light. To deny this fact is to deny yourself your creative expression of light. Each of us has our own creative endeavor of expression. We must not change ourselves to suit another if it is not our truth. To suppress our true expression would be to hold back our truth. To judge another for their form of expression is improper if that expression does not violate us or Universal Law. If an action does violate Universal Law, then the universe will provide the balance. If this action does violate our space, then it represents a part of our process and then must be dealt with. Otherwise, it is not our reality.

We all have a difficult period of adjustment ahead of us now. I say this because now we will all be held to and pressed forth with our truth. What we have been is the energy of who we are. Nothing can change this truth. I will also say that we all now will have the opportunity to take this truth and mold it with our heart as we see fit. To take these energies of culmination coming to us, the ones that are ours, and truthfully own and embrace them. Accept them, feel them in our heart, and then redirect them to reveal our core truth and reality. To have the courage to face ourselves, and accept our truth of reality, and then be bold enough to grow with it. To have the faith that our Creator, no matter what, is large and in charge always.

Now is the time for each of us to do our part in relation to our truth as it is appropriate in our life. To see and understand our truth and then be responsible for our truth. For this to happen, there must be a dedication to self of self-empowerment and self-illumination. There must be the honesty to see and accept our truth along with the will and faith to express our truth always.

The best way we can help others now will be to let them see how it is done. This is all a very personal process, an inside job, teaching by representation. Each soul will receive the necessary energetic outline and frequency appropriate for its soul growth outline, and living our truth with faith is the key.

For each of us, our truth is our only responsibility. To step out of our energetic profile of truth would mean to have judgment, doubt, fear, and a lack of faith in our ability and our creator's ability.

Through our heart and soul, creation reveals to each of us our part and role of cocreation with creation. We each then must respect and honor our heart and soul's reality of truth. As this directive of feeling comes forward to us, we each must then respond to this truth of our reality. To openly embrace it and empower it with our life expression and then reflect it for all to witness.

To live and express our truth with love completely at all times and under all circumstances is to never hold back our truth from its expression, generating imbalance. In living in this manner, all people will bring forth a very high and clear level of life, society, and reality, for all.

This new responsibility to self allows the heart and soul to open and share with us at higher and higher levels of empowerment from within, bringing each of us forward on our journey of life to experience more...

More Beauty, Balance, Power, Wisdom, Love,
and Grace on Our Stairway to Heaven.

Birthing Star

Chapter 2

The Shift

As we all embrace these energies of completion coming to all of reality now and live our heart and soul's truth openly, this now begins to become our normal daily routine of life. This process includes time as a direct energy component. The aperture of time will now open and expand its level of structure in relation to and with these new nonlinear frequencies we are experiencing, putting all creation in a state of flux. This means change for all. Everyone will be challenged in each and every moment to deal with new forms of reality.

The energy of this new way of life will be different for all. There will be great changes in our reality of physical form for each of us, and for our planet. The energies of this new creative cycle we are entering will be expanding for a great length of time. The energetic reality of creation and consciousness is accelerating now, humanity and creation will rise with it. I refer to this period now as the shift.

Since everything is comprised of energy, if the level of light of these energies of creation increases, then all of creation within its structure will rise to meet this new level of light. These new changes coming will be intense for all. This is because the fundamental building blocks of energy that our entire world, that we as a human race were built with, are expanding their atomic structure.

We are moving to a higher, clearer energy frequency light band. All aspects of creation will either shift with these frequency changes or will not. It can only be that way; there is no middle ground any longer. This shift is on all levels everywhere for everyone and everything.

This shift applies to our four bodies of expression—physical, mental, emotional, and most of all, spiritual. All creation that will not or cannot move from the old lower light frequencies to these new light energies will dissipate. All creation will either be empowered and uplifted or be redirected to another dimension of light in this new energetic forum. This is the case now with many aspects of our current life and world condition now.

This shift we are all in now has five aspects of creative force.

These shifts are:

a) Completion and Cleansing
b) Realignment
c) Harmonic Unity
d) I AM Synthesis
e) Cocreation

So here we all go…

Completion and Cleansing

There has been a good deal of information discussed in chapter 1 about completion. All of chapter 1 applies here now and from now on.

Do not put those feet up; put them firmly on the ground. Ground yourself and prepare yourself. Just as the mother bird knows when the baby is ready, she then releases her child to either take flight or fall. Many, with a bounce or two, make it. Some do not. We will all now be held accountable for ourselves and have to stand on our own two feet. Creation is pushing us all out of the nest. We each must shake off our old restraints and controls that have been discussed previously in *The Presence*. Put the key of faith in the ignition of our heart, and rise up to new heights of consciousness, enlightenment, empowerment, and illumination.

Our cleansing is in relation to all light frequency that is obsolete and no longer serves these new energies of creation. The Nemesis Star System, with Planet Nibiru coming into alignment with our solar system now, is providing a very dense magnetic energy field that will, let us say, delete many of the old limiting energy programs of power and control. These magnetics coming with the Nemesis Star System into our star system will be a game changer for our current reality. They will affect everything. They are the reason for our so-called global warming, since Nibiru and its high field of dense lower-field magnetics is heating up all the planets at their core level. As it arrives, our orbital pattern will shift, our tectonics will move, electronics will fry, and a wave of dark matter will pass over us all. The magnetics from this star system are very powerful and will set off and create many shifts of all kinds on our planet.

Its presence will also activate our other pole from inactivity to activity, creating many diverse new energy alignments that will seem very chaotic at first, but provide much more stability and empowerment for humanity once all is aligned and in balance again. We as a people on our planet will cease to war when this occurs. Very soon, we will all have to work together and unite to move forward with these changes coming for all. As President Reagan once said, maybe something from space will bring all the people of our planet together and unite them.

The interface of these two star systems will provide a great cleanse for humanity, Mother Earth, and our solar system. Those of us that make this shift will have a great responsibility and opportunity to cocreate our new world. As this world is in her period of realignment, we will all naturally have to work together to restore and rebuild. This will take brotherhood, patience, and love, not power and control or dollars and cents.

As these two solar systems reunite, they will reenergize and repolarize each other. The lower-field energies of Nibiru will assimilate all like matter. This is what I am calling "the clean sweep." Much like wiping a computer, which will also take place for all the electronics on this planet. Our new energetic fortifications will come from within. All creation on Planet Earth, our solar system, and beyond, will be realigned, recalibrated, and illuminated within a new frequency of light-energy magnetics.

A New Cycle Will Begin… A New Earth Will Be Formed…
The Seventh World of Creation Will Begin…

The Age of Attunement

Realignment

The realignment we will all go through now will be from the ground up and the inside out. This is a process that has occurred before and will occur again, but not at this frequency of light. We will all be in the same boat, so to speak. What I mean by this is that all the souls that can bridge these new frequencies and make this shift will enter this new reality. All souls that will not or do not make this shift will be realigned to their proper place of learning and growth. Many souls will need the experience of numerous incarnations to find their way. We are all now on a journey of faith in the moment, traveling forward with creation's new expression of reality coming forth for all of us now. No one will be left out of this journey of faith, love, and light.

Faith will be our guiding star, our key. I will say the greatest component of all will come from creation as the feeling of love, light, and perfection our creator will hold for us all now on this new journey of light's expression and expansion. Those souls that have made this transition have done so on their own merit. There is no free ride on our spiritual path. This is especially true at higher levels of learning, such as we are moving onto now.

This realignment process encompasses a great deal of time. It will involve the physical reconstruction of our planet, the development of new levels of state and society. New design and energy concepts of creation and learning, and all the while adapting ourselves to a less linear and higher dimension of physical reality.

Our field of influence from creation will now be a higher dimensional field of reality. All aspects of life itself will change. The cutting edge of reality that will be created will be brand new in an etheric physical crystal light energy field.

Harmonic Unity

For peace to prevail and exist on Planet Earth, it will require all souls to love and respect each other at our core level of being. In today's world, created from fear, judgment, and greed, this is impossible. Here and now on Planet Earth, it is very obvious that there are many people who have very definite agendas and goals for our reality and existence on this planet. They are using the energies of creation for power and control. This is not an acceptable reality any longer. The initial changes that are coming for the planet and her people are great in scope. They will provide a balance for this sphere of influence that we are currently not experiencing. This shift we are all in now is the beginning of the energetic realignment that is coming for all of creation from our creator.

All souls entering this next cycle will carry with them the light encodement of creation to be able to achieve this condition of reality. These energies are very active already and are waking up many of the souls designated to move forward into this new cycle. They will all walk with a strong desire and ability to encompass and adhere to these new realities of creation. This will involve a great deal of faith, harmony, and unity for a great length of time. The world as a whole will know its new reality and know there must be unity and brotherhood for all to prevail. All will have to give what they can and receive what they need.

This new period of conditioning will ease humanity into its new level of reality and unity that will create a free society. This new society will only acknowledge all of the highest attributes of life. It will encompass these attributes always and in all ways: honesty, harmony, integrity, pureness, balance, wisdom, truth, love, light, and grace. Right and wrong will be known to all. A new way of life from the ground up, on and with our mother of form, Mother Earth.

Our new progression of life will encompass our feeling body and emotional body to a greater and greater degree. When any imbalance is felt and known, it will provide discomfort for all immediate souls in that energetic vicinity. Everyone in these new frequencies will have the ability to read and feel all energy patterns and profiles if necessary.

As with any and all codes of conduct, there will be proper and improper ways to do this and for each person to experience each other's light field.

There will be rules of conduct on a similar level to the ones society has always had, only now they will be at a much higher level of love with respect.

I AM Synthesis

Heart and soul. We each have a heart, and we each have a soul. Some have sold theirs and would like to get it back. I will not name any names. For those of you that have, I am praying for you. My words of comfort are as follows: all roads lead home, some just take a little longer. All of the energies of creation serve our creator. We are all our creator's creation, and in existing, we are in service. I will be sixty-three in two weeks. I find the more I grow, the more I learn, the less I know. One foot in front of the other... It is a journey of life, of light, and of creation. On the other hand, I find more peace, more beauty, and nature is so amazing. The peace of creation in the moment with nature... So what is the end of our road? When do we get there?

As we all begin to find our peace and our beauty in each present moment on this beautiful, wonderful planet filled with nature's wonders once again in our new Earth's higher dimensional field of light.

I wonder...

In these new fields of living light, our hearts will open and expand their lotus blossom to receive a complimentary essence of love and light from our soul and from creation.

Our soul body of light has been waiting patiently and guiding us on our journey of light. Now even in the beginning of this cycle of living light, walking with an open heart with our soul light body.

Even in the beginning of this new reality. I wonder again, *When do we get there?* Well, I think we will all be well on our way. Well on our way of becoming one with ourselves, one with our soul, and one with our creator. This takes us all on a new journey of relationship and cocreation. Well on our way, for with our soul connection and empowerment, we open the door for relationship with creation. We then begin to become the God-self within and the I AM presence of creation.

The Age of Aquarius will begin with all souls taking on new levels of communication, learning, relationship, empowerment, and cocreation. It will be a wondrous time of life's expansion. We will all be learning together, working together, and building our new world together. A world filled with the highest of dreams and the purest of thoughts, all felt and known unto each other. All in the Key of Love…

So *I* before *E* except after *C*? How about no *I* and only We, then We All See.

For each soul to empower itself unto its I AM presence, bringing forth the I in I AM, then we each become a positive steadfast component of creation. As each of us becomes steadfast, whole, unified aspects of creation, then together as We, We become the new building blocks for reality and creation to expand.

Cocreation

Humanity has been in a partnership with creation since the beginning of its reality. Each step of the way, growing, evolving, and becoming more empowered. So here comes into play the big word, *Power*. First, you get the power, and then you dictate it. Pretty simple, yes? And very necessary for the parameters of reality that have existed.

So yes, we have been cocreating on many levels, energies of creation from all the machines we have built to all the medical wonders for our bodies. They have taught us a lot and empowered humanity greatly. But nothing ever seems to be enough, and our society strives for more constantly.

People are so enamored with their worldly issues and devices. They have no time or connection with their source, their creator, or with creation itself.

We can all see on some level now that the energies of power and control are becoming unnecessary in our modern-day world.

Well, yes, we can see it, we can desire it, but there are too many souls that carry too much imbalance for over too long of a period of time for that to exist right now.

Cocreation with our creator requires souls that have cleared their emotional body of imbalance to a degree that lets them open their heart and soul to receive our creator's love and light.

In this manner, we open the doorway of empowerment through our soul with creation. This is the difference in reality of life that this next cycle of light is bringing forward for all of humanity that this current cycle has lacked. You can label them cause and effect energies of creation, but they have been an integral aspect of learning for this past cycle.

Now as the souls that have evolved enough are waking up, it is becoming quite clear that this shift and spiritual awakening is really occurring right now.

So all we have to do is clear our timeline and clear our emotional field, and then we become enlightened? Good question, but not exactly. At that point in time, we open the door to begin our journey of empowerment with our core soul energy light field coming forward now in an energetic union, like a friendship.

This is deep and delicate...

The chakra energy centers all working together in alignment and attunement with our core soul level energy light field. So yes, this is the beginning stage of enlightenment. Many assume that enlightenment is instantaneous. There are many levels and aspects to empowerment and enlightenment.

This all comes to us on the road and journey of life. It is a never-ending process. So now I refer to this new time as the kindergarten of the Aquarian Age.

And a new school begins...

Some of the souls moving forward now onto this new light plane are highly evolved and have been preparing for this period of creation for eons of time. All that is occurring now on this planet has been known and prepared for a great deal of time.

Even these old souls will have a tremendous learning curve in this new reality of time and space. This is because all the souls and Mother Earth will now be unified in a new unique energetic light-field dimension of form. This is the next step on our path of enlightenment, empowerment, and cocreation of reality. The big change now is there will no longer be a separation of humanity from its soul body. Now that gap is closing.

The I AM presence, our Soul, is coming forward now for those who are ready.

This means to say that for those souls who are ready, their soul will actually unite with them to the degree that they are ready. To become one. To not be separate any longer. This next cycle will be for those that have made this shift to now develop a union with their soul body of light and walk together in form. This is why I refer to this age of creation as the Age of Attunement. All Creation growing and evolving together as One.

One with our Light-Body...

Attuning and evolving our light frequencies in each house of learning in our Zodiac of Creation, empowering and embodying them.

Just imagine how we might all be and what this Earth might look like after twenty-six thousand years of love, light, and perfection with our I AM presence and with our Creator.

We all are headed into a new arena of creation. All creation will be aligned within their proper energy light field of influence. Heaven or Hell? Well, it is really not as black-and-white as that. Let us just say different schools of light for each level of light. The essence of this new reality of existence for creation is incomprehensibly, incalculably, enormously expansive and will be a total game changer for all.

A Time to Live Our Truth...
To Shine Our Light Bright...

Star of Unity

Chapter 3

Acceptance

In discussing acceptance, we need to look at the many faces of the realities that we all need to have acceptance of. For this chapter, I will classify them as four different kinds of acceptance we need in our lives right now.

    a.   Acceptance of the past and present moment
    b.   Acceptance of self
    c.   Acceptance of the end of this cycle
    d.   Acceptance of this new Aquarian age

Acceptance of the Past and Present Moment

Acceptance begins and ends on the inside of each and every one of us. It is the correlation of our mind, heart, feeling, and soul body in a combination of energies that denote our reality feeling and belief of what it is that we are deciding to accept or not to accept in our lives as our reality. All people have their parameters of acceptance. These are our boundaries that we set up for each and every aspect of our lives. This is all very individual for each and every one of us.

There are new conditions of life that many people do not agree with, and are having to accept these realities that provide conflict for them and, let us say, a nonacceptance or nonapproval of these realities. Many people feel they must resign themselves to the reality that they must live with these realities that are nonacceptable.

Now we, each of us in this situation of our current reality, do have the one and only option we always have. To know our boundaries of acceptance, and live them as best we can. To express our truth openly and appropriately. To know and embody our truth of what it is that crosses our boundaries, and empower that aspect of ourselves always.

Now holding our truth right in our heart, we wear it openly, strongly, secure, yet still with love. The more we accept a nontruth and personal infringement, the more we condone it and thereby empower it. By giving it our energy, we keep it alive.

So here now, right now, things like chemical trails in the sky, vaccines for people that are now mandatory, worldwide systems of power and control, what can we do? We make our feelings known to those expressing their controls on us. We hold our faith, energizing our prayers with our love's essence secure in a clear light so as not to energize any of these energies that are nonacceptable with anger and hate. Even in the face of adversity, our truth, faith, love, and light will carry us forward to higher realms of light, no matter what the outcome physically. This requires courage. Remember, we are creator beings. We create our reality with our mind's reality of our heart's soul. *Abracadabra*—I create as I speak. Our creator created us to be creators also. It is time for each of us to use our creative energies to bring forth truth, love, and balance to our world…to not draw the sword.

I call this our living truth of reality. This is where we each have a very definite set of energy boundaries that will not ever be crossed. It is the acceptance and empowerment of the self. It is individual, it is ours, no one else owns it or has power over it, *period*. It is our living truth.

In these new apertures of light, there will be many new freedoms, but also new and very definite boundaries that must not be crossed. Those that are crossed will be dealt with in accordance with the inappropriate energy that was expressed. Nothing will be able to hide from these new parameters of light coming forth now. This is also why so many hidden truths that have been held for eons of time are coming forth now into the light to be expressed openly.

These new energy frequencies demand expression. Like a truth serum. No one can resist. No one and nothing, all the energies of form will now express themselves openly.

Once again, faith, hope, love, and grace are our keys to the kingdom of light. To be or not to be? It is not a question any longer. It is now a mandate of time, space, and reality.

We each now must choose our path, our position, and our reality. Acceptance has many faces, and many realities. A big part and probably the biggest part for all now is the acceptance of the real in reality around what has been created on Planet Earth.

As the dark side of our reality expresses itself openly, acceptance of the way this world has been and still is in so many ways, is what we each must have now. We cannot pretend all this darkness does not exist. But also, we should not condemn or condone it. In our new relationship with creation, we are only responsible and accountable for self. Being whom we are, empowering ourselves, our own master of self. When and if we are called forth to perform beyond self, it will be felt and known.

There are lower and higher realms of light just as we each have lower and higher energy fields in our body. Lower vibrations, such as anger, hate, fear, power, and control support and empower the lower realms energetically. They supply energy that supports and empowers them. This is why it is important for us not to empower them with our energy frequencies by responding and reacting to them. Our upper vibrations such as peace, harmony, tranquility, love, and light support and empower the upper fields of love and light. Both these energy fields are energies of creation, energies of love and light. We all now must choose one side or the other for our final expression of the finalization of this cycle.

This will not always be an easy process. Many changes will occur in a brief period. We will all need to hold ourselves to our living truth as best we can in the days ahead.

Faith Is Our Key… Love Is Our Power…

Acceptance of Self

There has been a great deal of discussion around the parameters of self, and how we each can apply our energies in the most appropriate manner. This has all been very positive, and I am sure you each have other thoughts and feelings to apply that are empowering also. Faith is a very big asset here for all, as are all the angels always. So this is all great and wonderful. But where does it leave you? Yes, you, the one reading this right now. You, the one having a big problem trying to wrap your head around this material. Trying to find your connection and feeling in this moment. So now what are the magic words? Well, I am writing this, and I am wondering right now what these magic words are also. This is my present moment because I am not sure what I will say next.

So now after sitting here for a few minutes, it finally just came to me. To my feeling and into my body. The answer for us all is the Human Spirit. Our soul, our energy of creation, that spark of life, that fire of light. Faith, yes faith, but also the knowing. The knowing that being whom we are is everything and the only thing empowering that spark our creator has given each of us. What I am talking about is that fire from creation that makes us invincible. The strength that lets you pick up a car to save your child. The love of a good person that will bring you back from the edge of disaster and death. The Holiday Light that shines in everyone's eyes…

These are essences of that spark that every human being has and cannot be taken away. We each must find ours and set it on fire with the flame of life, the human spirit. Somehow, each of us has to find this part of ourselves and empower it. This is the aspect of each of us that gets us through those really tough times when you feel like you are going to die but somehow you pull it back together. We all have had a moment like this when our Creator talks to us. Like when a song just for you comes on the radio right at the right moment when you are missing your mother, and it was her favorite song. Or when a stranger comes and gives you a message, and it was exactly the answer you were looking for, and he had no idea what you were feeling. We must accept ourselves always as much as we accept our creator and creation itself.

I wish to share a true story here with all. Years ago, I was assisting my mother, who had terminal cancer, with my crystals. I use crystals, color, and sound to help the body balance and heal. While sharing with my mother, my grandmother, who had passed long before, came to give me a message for my mother. It was an intense moment working with my mother and trying to hold the space for her without judgment. My grandmother kept saying, "I have a message for Ruthy." And I said, "Okay, Grandma." This was all telepathic and not out loud.

I was not really used to telepathic messages and also I was really concerned for my mother's mental outlook since this was the first time I had shared energy with her in this manner. My grandmother, Catherine ("Kitty"), kept saying to me to tell her the message. Well, this went on for about fifteen minutes, and by this time, Kitty was saying to me "Tell her" in a very loud manner. My mother was doing really well and receiving a lot of wonderful energy. The room was electric.

So when Grandma Catherine yelled at me that last time, I knew I could not dismiss her any longer. I quietly said to my mother, "Mom, Grandma is here, and she has a message for you. The message is, 'Even though I was not the best mother, I still love you very much.'" So there, I had relayed the message. My mother continued her energy session without a word or even opening her eyes. I was on my toes at this point. I was not sure what was going on. But I held my faith. I was running completely on faith. It was all I could do to hold myself together. A very emotional time for me.

We finished our time, and my mother began to get grounded enough to sit up. She told me she had a wonderful journey. She was not sure where she had gone but said that it was very beautiful, and she felt very good. I knew she had gone through a lot, especially for this being her first time and also her being so ill. I just held the space of love and faith that everything was in divine order without hardly saying a word, just supporting her now in that present moment. I had coached her at the beginning of this session on a guided journey. But now, after all that occurred, I held my tongue and let her have the space that was provided. I was not sure if she even heard what I said to her.

After about an hour, as she sat quietly, she looked at me and said, "Clifford, I got to my mother's side twenty minutes after she had passed. I went into her room and sat beside her. I was the only one in the room. I felt my mother's leg. It was still warm. I then leaned over and looked into her big blue eyes. I whispered in her ear, 'Even though you were not the best mother, I still love you very much.'"

My mother told me this, and said to me, "Clifford, I have never told another living soul about this ever."

At that point, I felt very good inside. It was a very wonderful experience that I will never forget.

When we each can accept the fact of who we are, and hold that faith and never let go. Then the music of life plays for us. A single moment can change our lives if we have enough faith and acceptance in our present moment. Creation is looking for ways to support each of us always, but first, we each must fulfill our part and role in creation. We each must be accountable to ourselves and be there with enough love and faith in each present moment to be able to receive our creator's love and support on our journey of light. How can we receive support if we are not open and trying also?

My mother's cancer went into remission, and she passed on March 9, 2023, at the age of ninety. As I lay sleeping early morning March 10, I heard my birth name, Clifford, being called out to me over and over very softly but soon awoke. My mother was calling me, and when I awoke, she said, "Clifford, this is your mom. I want you to know that even though I was not the best mother, I still love you very much." She told me how happy she was to be out of that old body and many other wonderful things that morning. I could not believe that the reality of this story of love and family ties in my life had progressed full circle and now was being represented to me in my life as a new truth for me to accept. I was so grateful for this new vision of reality that was brought to me that day, and for the new life my mother had received...

Acceptance of the End of This Cycle

Many people in life on this planet have no idea of all the changes that are happening now. They do not want to know either. They do their best to be an ostrich and keep their heads down. Even those who consider themselves open and aware are very uninformed about the reality of this world. This book will put me on the edge of it all. I am not sure how this will go. I pray my words help those that desire to see a little more light on this whole process. In March of 2017, NASA released information that it discovered an asteroid, which they nicknamed Bennu, that was on a collision course with Earth and would be here in ninety years.

Our government has been building underground bases for a very long time. They have them all across the country with underground highways also. There is also the world seed bank that looks like a fortress. So this is as far as I go out on this limb. My reason for this is because there are enough books on these topics. What I am writing is meant to empower us all, not to bring up fear.

With all these facts alone, we can all see major change in the forecast for our planet, let alone all the change we see right now. So now back to acceptance. Yes, to now have it at all levels as much as we can feel it. To empower ourselves from within as best we can. Those that go boldly forth usually make it to the other side of their goal. The Nemesis Star System and our solar system will be aligning soon with each other. This alignment will redirect all matter into a new energy profile and set our solar system on a new course back into our universe and the houses of the zodiac. We will all begin a new cycle of light. There will be major changes and shifts of the tectonic plates, and our Earth will have a new look to it as this shift completes itself. All matter will realign itself in this new energy format. Acceptance of the changes that are occurring now is mandatory.

We each must honor ourselves and our brothers and sisters by empowering ourselves from within, keeping a cool head, and holding a strong faith with a positive outlook. Holding faith in our creator, putting our best foot forward, and knowing we are eternal, immortal, universal, and infinite aspects of creation is our cocreative position right now. We have all lived multiple lives and will continue to until we all finish our journey of light and return home to be one with our Creator.

Acceptance of the Aquarian Age

People are still talking about their 401(k). This world is coming apart at its seams. And all this is totally appropriate. The ministers on TV, the politicians in office, the news companies debating each other in a world without ethics or morals. Just like the days of Sodom and Gomorrah all over again. Turn off your TV sets. Throw them out the window. I like the old school monster movies where the world cannot get along with each other, but then there's a space invader, and all of a sudden, we all work together and become allies again. Our universe is comprised of many realities of creation, but the real evil that threatens us all right now is right here on Planet Earth.

So just as the energies of light are all around us always providing energy for our cocreative process, also in reciprocal to this, the lower or dark energies are right there too. They are both omnipresent, ready to serve us. Especially right now at this moment of culmination of this cycle, tempting each of us to their corner.

So what does all this acceptance mean right now? To look at this out-of-balance world and to see it as it is, rather than what it is not, and accept it. To feel all our energies of life and creation with our spark of life in acceptance, to accept the fact that all is changing now, as it has many times before, and we each will express our love, light, and truth about it. And last but not least, to accept, know, and have the faith that our creator will bring us forward into the next level of creation as always before. With all of this, the magic of creation expands once again. Aquarius beckons us all now. How perfect to set up our New World in Aquarius.

People everywhere, especially the young people, are breaking away from this current world. They do not care for the world that they were born into, so they are building their own. They would rather live as vagabonds than to join today's society. They see the redundancy of this whole reality and refuse to be a part of it. People all over the globe are waking up and questioning this current reality. They are introducing new higher ideals for existence and are refusing to follow the old systems. They question all these systems that have existed. They question everything. The lower realms of power and control are losing ground every day as they begin to shift forward into the light too. Their purpose is to provide a reflective balance energetically, but only as long as it is necessary. Their energies of creative capacity will evolve and expand as the children of light move forward into the light. They will shift and expand to maintain the balance from behind as time and space evolve energetically forever.

The energies of light of this new age of light we are entering will be the driving force of change for all of creation now. As the trees in the forest fall, their seeds have already sprouted. People everywhere now are changing. The world is changing its ideas and its ideals. Rather than cling to the old ways of this world that are in dysfunction, we must instead let them go to embrace these new energies of creation. To be our piece of the pie. We each must put aside and release from our energy field all that is of dysfunction and judgment. We each must open our heart and soul to this new level of light and level of life.

I have one main purpose in my life right now. That purpose is to assist everyone in finding their own inner truth, faith, love, light, and express it with as much love as possible on their journey of light, just as I am finding it, expanding it, and embodying it, more every day myself. I guess you could say the Nemesis Star System is the space invader. It will provide the changes that are needed in many ways. It actually is our savior on a great level. As these star systems interface, it will discharge Earth's lower magnetic field. This is where all of the lower, dark energy is held. These are the energies of the powers that have been in control of this planet over this last cycle. So Planet Nibiru will actually clear our energy field of many of these lower frequencies, allowing more light to come to the Earth plane. This will release Mother Earth and humanity from the energies of darkness that have been in control of this planet for eons of time dimensionally to some degree, while generating a new dimension of light without polarity for those that are ready on Mother Earth.

Our acceptance on all levels of our self, our Creator, and creation itself as this transition occurs will assist each soul to hold its precious present moment of time and space and shift with these changes to the degree of their light embodiment, moving in sync in and with the completion and realignment of this cycle of creation into our next cycle of creation.

The Nemesis Star System and Planet Nibiru will clear the field for us and create a space for a great deal more light to come to Planet Earth for the next cycle of creation and the Age of Aquarius.

Gateway Star

Chapter 4

Regeneration

To each will be given our tools of freedom. To use to find ourselves, to build, to rebuild, to empower, to expand, to illuminate, to endow, to release, to live, and to love… As all these energies of culmination surge forth, we each bear witness to all of creation. The new light of day is allowing us all to see the necessity for change and feel the one coming. Our brothers and sisters are all striving to maintain their lives and some form of balance. We are all in a recalibration of life. Everyone sees this change happening. Many are trying to repair our world and keep going on with life as we have always done before in a period of crisis.

This regeneration I am speaking of now is an energy process of expansion. Many talk about the end of times. They look at the glass of water as to whether it is half full or half empty. They still only see a glass of water. I see the energies of creation living in the moment. First of all, that glass could become anything, maybe turned into a glass angel, and that water could evaporate, be frozen, and turned into snowflakes of all kinds. I might wonder how many beautiful snowflakes there were in that angel.

Okay, fun, huh! Well, that is all still 3D stuff,
so let us all go a little further okay?

Remember the energies of creation, omnipresent in the present moment, where with enough faith, self-discipline, self-empowerment, and self-enlightenment, we begin to become our master of self.

The masters of self, even in the old limited 3D frequencies, were able to levitate, create form from thought, turn water into wine, heal the sick, and share wisdom, love, and grace with humanity. They were open to expand with creation and not be limited by it. In these new frequencies of light, with new higher levels of creation coming forward for all of existence, all matter will shift and regenerate with it.

Over this last cycle, many different civilizations were created in many different fields of influence in different houses of the zodiac. They each had one thing in common. They all took place within the same energy cycle of creation. Now this energy process of creation is beginning again and in the same manner which has happened before. The one main difference is that this new cycle will occur in a new higher octave of color and sound.

As the color and sound frequencies expand their fields higher and lower, this changes the frequency resonance of reality. These new expanded energy fields of reality are changing the molecular structure of reality. This fact alone denotes a restructure and regeneration of all matter. As I have already mentioned, this new field of light is the reason so many systems of our current reality no longer function properly.

Now back to the glass of water. A master of self and a master of light would be able to see, feel, and drink a wonderful full glass of water or have it become whatever the present moment necessitated.

The regeneration of our world and society will be an intense process for all. Every aspect of creative force will be active at the same time. Some energies will culminate, expand, blossom, and bear fruit while others dissipate. Landmasses will rise from the depths of the oceans to reveal themselves and their hidden treasures while others that have been soiled will recede to be cleansed. This regeneration will have many faces of reality to it.

Our mother of form will regenerate herself anew in a very similar fashion just as her children of form regenerate themselves. All matter of form, all energy of thought, all energy of emotion, and the energy of spirit itself will now take on new parameters of frequency of existence in form. All this change will be a work in progress.

Many aspects of our creative process will change and expand in the reality and diversity of their level and reason for creation. New and exciting forms of energy and energy tools will be coming soon. Some of them are here now but have been hidden from humanity. There will be fast, efficient new ways to create and maintain this new world we will all build together.

The regeneration of all matter has already begun.

We must all face the fact now that these energies of recalibration, realignment, and recreation are here now. We are all in a high field of flux, which means change. I meet people every day who are struggling with their reality and their emotional body.

The reason for this is all our energies of imbalance are being brought to the surface to be expressed. This is happening to all people everywhere and will continue until the Earth plane is free of limitation at this frequency of creation for this next level of light to transpire and begin. It has already begun, but the actual shift has not taken place yet.

This shift will occur when the Nemesis Star System and Planet Nibiru pass by us in its orbital cycle. The reason I have written these books is to assist all on their journey of expansion.

We all have a great opportunity right now to make great strides and amass more light right now. On some level, you can relate this period right now to that period of high school or college when you took your final exams or wrote your thesis. I remember in my high school, if you passed your final exam, you passed the course. I would relate this time we are all in to a similar condition. So you can see that this is a very important, intense, brief period at the end of this great cycle of creation we have all been a part of. Each will receive what they need in accordance with their directive of creation.

Soon the entire planet will know of this change coming. There will be a mass awakening to this fact.

This shift of reality will spark the greatest human energy release ever. It will be vast and overwhelming.

Many souls are being energetically aligned to be unaffected and remain stable during this shift and the days to come. Many will be at a loss as to what they should do to prepare themselves for whatever they believe the outcome of it all will be.

Now the energies of creation are coming to each of us to ask us who we are, testing all souls on the planet now as to who they are. All souls on the planet now are being asked who they are. Testing our mettle, so to speak.

To regenerate means to take what has been and re-empower it with new vitality that brings forth more than there was before. Our Creator is asking each of us who we really are, allowing everyone through the expression of life to show our true colors and expand with them.

Now as we all integrate our timeline of expression of form, we are coming into frequencies of extreme change to challenge each of us as to our real truth.

Many who have not met their challenge well before will now have a unique opportunity to shine their light in a new and glorious manner.

What I am saying is that this regeneration beginning now is an opportunity for many to shine in a new way, to take their reality of light embodiment and advance and empower it greatly.

A pivotal point in creation for our creator to witness our frequencies of light in action. Revealing who we each are in this New Light to witness those that have shined brightly and those that have not, reveal all, and find new levels of themselves they were not aware of. The ability to shift and change in a moment of time and space in the blink of an eye.

To be able to access ourselves consciously on a new level and reequate that new wisdom and insight into the now of time and space.

I will share with all once again; my darkest hours provided me with my greatest light. Now we are all entering this black hole, wormhole, stargate… There are many names for different energy alignments.

This is the energy alignment.

A really big show… Ed Sullivan—Ed Sullyrock from *The Flintstones*. Well, where we are going in this new cycle compared to where we have been will make this last cycle look like the Stone Age of the Flintstones. A little humor goes a long way even in a dark hour, and even if you do not understand it. My definition of humor is this. *Hue-more*: "to add more color band light waves as we expand our energy body."

Back to our main theme here. In and with these new frequencies, regeneration will be the new order of the day. Our health and medical fields will change greatly. All of this frequency expansion will activate our DNA/RNA junk strands greatly. All our junk body parts will be activated for their true purpose. The human body was designed to expand with its light directive infinitely over time and space. These new light frequencies will allow the human body the ability to heal itself in many new ways, and to a much greater degree. Just as our current body receives two sets of teeth, there will be new energetic ratios on this level that will continue to expand well into the future of this cycle. As these energetic frequencies expand, their scope and ratio within this new cycle, all people everywhere will experience a much higher and longer level of life. This will all take place in accordance with our core energy field of light. The more light we carry and embody, the more we will each shift to fuller and longer levels of embodiment.

This will also be realized from the soul level of embodiment. In other words, we each will have our embodiment as long as it serves the soul empowerment and its alignment with creation.

As this cycle completes itself, each soul's energy outcome and final alignment of frequency energy body will denote its future energy profile and assignment, so to speak. As I have mentioned before, there are many reasons why souls incarnate in embodiment.

Since we are finalizing this cycle, many older souls will probably move to other assignments. Others are being aligned now to be ready to shift to take on leadership roles in this new cycle of light coming.

There are also many young souls that are here for the experience of this end of the cycle to add to their energy portfolio of experience.

Our world is in its process of regeneration...

We all now have a great opportunity to expand with this regeneration and shift onto these new higher fields of light emanating now from our Creator and from creation.

I invite everyone to open to expand your truth, your love, and your energies of creation, to be all that you can be, now and always.

Let Us Each Become a Master Tailor, Learning to Stitch
Together the Fabric of Time and Space on Our Journey
of Creation, Weaving Our Tapestry of Life.

Earth Star

Chapter 5

Unity

There is only one Earth. There are other planets, yes. But still there is only one Earth. A precious jewel of creation. A wonderful sphere of influence with so many life-forms of creation. A fabulous home our Creator provided for us all. It gives us our basis of form, embodiment, multiple life-forms for its homeostasis, and altogether a living, loving environment to expand our light.

This arena of light; earth, air, fire, water, color, sound, and spirit comprise our physical reality. Mother Earth and our Creator through many energies of creation work together as a unit. The forces of nature, the elemental kingdoms, the plant and mineral kingdoms, the nature kingdoms, and the animal kingdoms all have their place and maintain their pulse as a unit of creation.

The natural scope and position of our planet allow Mother Earth, under all circumstances, to maintain and balance herself always. Through the many changes she has been through, she always rebounds back to her balance and beauty because all her forces work together as cohesive units within a Unity of Existence.

This is a mandate of life for her to exist, and now it is becoming one for humanity also.

This past cycle of cause and effect energies that our planet has been through allowed humanity a great deal of leeway to create and destroy. Our new energies of creation coming forth now will not allow this to occur any longer. Those that will still create imbalance will pay a great penalty. The light coming to our solar system now is illuminating all of creation. It is revealing all: the good, the bad, and the ugly—right now, mostly bad and ugly.

From a pure energy of creative reality of this past cycle, the lower field expressions of creation were allowable and acceptable for the learning they provided, but no longer.

There are so many systems out of control. Imbalance is very apparent everywhere. There are world situations like Fukushima and the continents of garbage floating in our oceans, that no one talks of. Unity is the key component to help humanity now. Yet no one seems able to find the key—the key of life.

These energies of imbalance will be swept from our mother soon. As I have mentioned before, it is time now to create our own unit of light. To shine along with other units of light in Unity. To do our best each day, to shine our light and love of self in a unified way, adding unity and balance to our world, not emanating imbalance. Instead of the collective consciousness of 3D, we will have a new reality of unified fields of consciousness moving onto higher dimensions of nonlinear, non-polarized light.

Just as our mother of form, Mother Earth takes care of herself. She in turn teaches us all our responsibility to self. To maintain and empower ourselves in a positive cohesive energetic relationship with all of creation.

Our mother is her own master of self. We must become our own master of self. In this new cycle of creation, each soul will be accountable for all it creates on every level. Unity is a big piece of the pie of creation that has been missing for a long time. Just as the energy of truth will change this planet, the energy of unity will also. To be unified is the next level of life on Mother Earth. And she has been very patiently waiting.

In today's world, we can hardly get a room full of people to agree on anything. Sure, we get a poll or vote from a group of people that says they agree, but in reality, if they did actually talk to each other, it would end up in a dispute.

Right now, on this planet, these new energies of light are bringing everyone's personal truth to the surface to be expressed. Right, wrong, or indifferent, everyone is expressing what personal truth they have been holding. Everyone wants unity, but they also want their truth to be, *the Truth*. As I have said before, this is a time of culmination of all energy generated over this cycle. This all has to take place as this cycle ends. Nothing can stop this process from occurring. For unity to come, expression must take place. It is a part of our process right now.

All energy that has been suppressed and withheld throughout the timeline of creation over this past cycle of light is coming forward now to be expressed. This is true for those energies of creation that have been controlling and manipulating reality along the timeline and also during this period of creation for reasons of power and control. How, when, and where this will all take place will be different for all of us. All the energies of imbalance must be diffused for unity to take place. Our world is clearing, cleansing, and aligning in this process of expansion right now, trying to find Truth and trying to achieve Unity. We are all in this process of expansion now.

What I have been sharing so far is happening for our entire universe. All life-forms and all matter throughout the time and space of this cycle of our universe are in this process of completion. Getting our houses in order. Accountability, responsibility, truth, and unity are the order of the day. The energy of this period. This is all very true for the current energies of reality, and for our new reality and cycle that is coming closer to being our new form of life every day now. It is all a shift. Some days and experiences more abrupt than others. You could say a constant Mandela effect. Inevitably, it will be a constant level of growth. This is what our physical incarnation is all about now more than ever before.

Our current world and reality have the energies of power and control trying to establish their new world order, and one world. To have every person on this planet receive their chip and become a unit for the world order. They also want to bring the world under one form of leadership with a world currency. This is their form of unity. Totally controlled and manipulated from outside forces of power and control. Their new world order is from the outside. It is the mirror and reflection and opposite reality of our creator's plan holding the balance in reciprocity in their world. The fallen angels running the whole show. All we have to do is give up our god self, our soul, and pledge allegiance to them. Pretty simple stuff. There are a lot of people on this planet right now that are already doing this. This all has been going on for a very long period of time. They have done a really good job of removing our creator from our lives and putting themselves in our Creator's shoes.

Our Creator, on the other hand, is large and in charge. There is only one director's chair on the set of this movie, and our Creator sits in it. Everyone is in this movie taking place right now worldwide. And when the waters part once again, again only the righteous will be on the other side.

Creation's new cycle of light will be generated and run by the souls who embody the living light in open common energies of peace, love, and unity on all levels from within the hearts of all. In this next cycle, unity will come forward naturally from within the hearts and souls of humanity. From the inside of our core soul light field body in higher dimensions of living light. Unity is a necessary and common aspect of reality. Only when there are imbalances applied do we see problems occur. Unity is a common decency that all people everywhere really desire and put forth. Most people, for the common good, will work together.

As these new energies of light shine on humanity, many souls who are open are beginning to see and find new avenues of life and creation far above the old parameters of power, control, and greed. To live and work together as a unit in Unity supports everyone. There are two aspects of having Unity in our world. The first one is very isolated and individual. This refers to the singular form of unit or self. For in true Unity, each member or unit, accepting its role in supporting Unity, agrees to do its part. To fulfill its obligation of support in its part or role in the creative endeavor that is a part or piece in supporting the whole.

This soul would not only provide its creative energy expression but would also be responsible in all avenues of its life, which is also a part of supporting Unity and a cohesive life on and with our Mother in direct relation with creation. This role or part would be similar to a job today, but in our new world, just a way of life, expanding our light.

Now we shift from the singular of Unity to the plural. This part is where all souls energetically openly relate to and with each other. There are no hidden frequencies here, so there is clarity right from the start all the way to the finish. In any event, all will naturally apply their feelings openly and honestly. Even if there were to be an indecision reached, an elder of light would provide insight, or the majority would carry. In such a case, all other parties would then shift to the ultimate decision of support, balance, cohesion, and Unity.

The bottom line for all will be to have the best possible outcome on all levels for all creation. People will be thinking of all of creation when they make their decisions of creation.

This will be a different world for all to dwell in and on. Relationship will have a new parameter. All souls will have a strong connection with all creation naturally.

The beauty, harmony, and Unity of all of creation will bring a new and wonderful level of joy and light to our world. Unity is a very important part of reality for humanity.

A natural harmonic of Unity flowing from the heart and soul of Humanity, Mother Earth and Creation itself will allow an alignment of Light for all to behold...

A Wondrous Time of Creation.

Star of Expansion

Chapter 6

Harmony

A harmonious world will require all humanity to clear their emotional body of their power and control issues and create magnetic balance between the conscious personality and its soul essence. This is the "mechanics," you could say, the nuts and bolts of balancing the spiritual-physical reality.

When you get right down to it, emotion is just energy in motion in physical form. The big piece of our pie, that so many people cannot seem to get a hold of, is harmonizing and balancing their emotional body and keeping it that way.

In life, physically clearing our energy field or energy body of imbalance is our goal, to become our own master of self. We are all working through our energy issues and imbalances. It takes our so-called time for this to occur. Once again, this is not a mental process. It is a process of energy magnetics. You could say like harmonizing the cellular structure so that all cells coordinate with each other and do not create friction or adverse energy alignments.

This all sounds very easy. But, consider this point. We are in the process of finalizing this twenty-six-thousand-year cycle of incarnations in multiple civilizations. If you take a peek at our world and the people in it, you can see there is still a little room for improvement.

The seven major energy chakra body fields of energy have three centers above the heart and three below. As we shift into this next cycle, we step up in magnetics and begin to move away from a linear energy field of creation, opening the door for our energy field to engage more nonlinear energies of creation. Stepping onto nonlinear energy magnetics takes us away from polarity. This allows energy a new level of freedom.

Just as I have mentioned before, Mother Earth and her children of light will now utilize energy not only from our North Pole but also from our South Pole. This new energy ratio will only expand as we move through this new energy cycle. So now all seven chakras activated and running energy in multiple directions, all centered at our heart. With a clear and balanced energy body operating in a harmonious way, we then open the door to a real relationship with our core soul energy light-body. Our soul has always been there for us, allowing each of us our learning.

From time to time, it steps in and gives us a little push in the right direction. I have always called this my little voice. Well, I can tell you all, we all have a little voice. But few take the time to open the door to hear this voice and develop a relationship with it. We have all had a great deal of time to experience this linear time-mind feeling energy reality called 3D. So here now, a little more information about time and clearing our timeline.

When a judgment occurs, then there is a nonacceptance of something we experience in our energy field. Since we are creator beings, our judgment creates an energy interface with what we are judging. This interface relates back to us as time. Through our non-acceptance of a reality, we formulate our resistance to this reality and then lock this reality into existence through our non-acceptance and judgment. By judging, we actually help energize it by giving our energy to it. This judgment and nonacceptance actually feed it and energize it to stay in place as a part of our learning. We, through our judgment, become a part of the process itself.

Our creator provided this field of influence we now dwell in as a period for our growth, learning, and also to have and develop a relationship with ourselves along with time and space. These are energies that must be experienced and embodied to expand our energy portfolio.

Now as our linear 3D reality begins to expand its energy parameter to include nonlinear energies of creation, we are all feeling this expansion. As this aperture of time and space expands, this directly affects our conscious reality. Within the scope of our time and space, reality is moving to be less linear, expanding our aperture of consciousness to begin to feel, understand, and experience higher dimensions of light.

Our consciousness has been very limited for a great period of this past cycle of creation, keeping many aspects of reality hidden and unexpressed for the expressions of power and control as a part of our learning. As our aperture of light along with more nonlinear time and space frequencies expand, so does our consciousness. This all means energy will now flow more freely and less restricted. This is why all these energies of fear, power, and control are now being brought to the surface to be expressed openly.

Our planet, Mother Earth, and her children have lived in a controlled and manipulated sphere of influence for quite some time. All our lower fields of influence have provided many levels of learning throughout the time and space of this cycle. Through their direct and indirect energies of manipulation, they have greatly expanded humanity's energetic profile over many aspects of creation. Through these energy interactions, all souls have been tested and retested around their weakness and imbalance. They have served humanity well. For those of us who are ready, it is now time to move forward to higher levels of learning and empowerment.

As the Nemesis Star System and Planet Nibiru posture themselves towards us, their magnetics are literally heating up our planet. With all this heat emanating from our core and these high magnetics coming forward, by the time Planet Nibiru passes by us, the tectonics will shift, and the volcanoes will erupt even more than they are now.

There is a great deal of lower-field magnetics and magnetic fields held in place on our planet now. These magnetics are very dense. As Nibiru interfaces with Planet Earth and our solar system, there will be a great discharge of these lower field magnetics from our Earth and our solar system. During this interface and magnetic release, the Nemesis Star System and our solar system will shift to a like field of polarity and then repel each other back into a new trajectory and orbital pattern of the two binary star systems.

This discharge of dense lower-field magnetics will provide a great clearing for our solar system and Mother Earth. Since every aspect of creation is a form of energy, this magnetic discharge of lower-field magnetics will apply to all creation. This energetic discharge by both star systems will provide a balance of the energetic frequencies of magnetics between the two star systems. How this interface will end up is unknown. What I can say is that the more everyone can access their upper chakra field of magnetics will determine their next level of interface. Most of humanity will shift in body to new dimensions of reality while others will reincarnate when it is appropriate for their soul alignment in time and space. All other life-forms will align again energetically in body dimensionally or reincarnate again within their proper light field energy range of creation. The shifts of reality and consciousness that many have been noticing for quite some time are known as the Mandela effect. These shifts in reality dimensionally are already ongoing.

For Mother Earth and her children of light, a great weight will have been lifted. Upon the release of these dense frequencies of light, a great aperture and parameter of time and space will open to receive more light. This will revitalize all of creation in a new and wondrous way, allowing all lower fields of creation to be less dense, less rigid, and have more light, becoming more flexible.

This energy shift will bring all the energy fields of creation into a more unified field of influence, providing greater and greater harmony and balance. With so much density being released, consciousness will expand greatly. This will create many great new attributes for humanity, Mother Earth, our universe, and Creation itself.

With the release and shift of magnetics that will take place, along with the fact that our solar system is entering a higher field of light and frequency, the aperture of time and space of creation will expand greatly. This fact alone denotes a huge change in physical reality on all levels of creation. A lighter and brighter, less dense field of influence.

Our human biological bodies will take on these new and expanded energies, activating our dormant DNA/RNA encodement. The human body will lighten and expand itself, becoming more fluid and less dense. It will generate its own new energy light field connection and communication with the etheric light-fields we are entering.

This will be the basis of our new reality of being within our structure of existence. This will release humanity from its past profile of external stimulation and information to become an internal position of feeling and knowing. All life-forms entering this next octave of color, sound, and light will find themselves expanding continuously. Our new life-energy field of influence will be shifting and adjusting itself as it gradually rises and expands itself. A very cohesive and smooth up-leveling of light particle, frequency expansion, and integration. This will all happen automatically, and it will become our normal way of existence. Just as we grow from children to adults, we will all now begin again. The growth this time will be in conjunction with our soul light body.

This will all be a very busy, beautiful period of creation—the Wild West of the Aquarian Age. The big difference this time, of course, is that there will be no weapons or killing anymore. All people everywhere will discover new energies of creation at their fingertips with a thought and a feeling, communicating telepathically, especially with those close to you. There will be a clear and open understanding in regard to energy generation and assimilation by all. All people everywhere will have a very clear, open understanding of their creative energy expression and a great desire to fulfill it.

This all only empowers and expands the soul's energy portfolio. This promotes a high level of energetic symbiosis, emotional balance, and satisfaction. This would be a state of euphoria for all people everywhere as a normal state of being and reality of life. There are so many ways that this new world will be a wonderful place to live. All systems will employ the highest and best technology for all levels of creation. Any systems that outlive their technology will be recycled and reorganized energetically.

No products of any kind will be made worldwide with substandard, non-approved building materials and packaging products. All of creation from start to finish will have a proper energy alignment of function. There will not be countries any longer. There will be quadrants of creation. There will be no language barriers as we all begin to communicate telepathically. There will not be multiple manufacturers trying to get your business. There will be no money or economical system. All products will be generated in the most positive and appropriate manner. There will be no piles of garbage. Everything made will be requalified in the appropriate manner. There will be no true ownership, although everyone will have what they need when they need it. If you think about it, we do not own anything now really. We just get to use things for a period of time.

I would say, in these new frequencies, we would all be closer to a true level of real ownership. Also, we will live longer and have more time to enjoy this world as we expand our energy light fields intrinsically.

This new world will all work together separately. Each a part of the whole. Each a separate snowflake. Each snowflake able to expand its horizon of light as it sees fit in balance with the world. Just as faith is the key, now too comes balance in the movement through time and space. Faith with balanced harmonics in the present moment of time and space.

So now as we move forward with our new beautiful world, we each do what we love, as our Selective Energy Expression. As long as this serves us well, if not we go to our SEER—Selective Energy Expression Representative—and generate a new SEE—Selective Energy Expression. We then go to our beautiful home. Our dwelling is easily maintained, and a very versatile place of regeneration, self-generation, private relationship, and private retreat. Most of our extracurricular items, such as bikes, boats, kayaks, except for those items we chose to keep for daily activity, will be accessible at our local activity center.

Our modern homes will have kitchens of course, but they will be small because our energy intake will be simple and there will be many established nourishment centers for all to utilize any time everywhere. All systems for life on all levels are provided always. There are different structures and types of places to dwell all over the planet. All one would have to do to relocate would be to apply to a section coordinator.

Each and every soul will have personal and vacation time that is generated, which will be far greater than that of this reality. My feeling is each soul would have at least one week for every two months of expression. Also, the expression conditions would be very upgraded, to provide tranquility and empowerment under all conditions. Hours would be very flexible depending on energetic creative dynamics. There will be quite a bit of automation, but in a clean way. All systems of SEE will employ proficient energy-ratio applications of time and space from every aspect of the reality of creation, in other words, balance of life.

Our new world will have crystal energy centers worldwide that would be located at crystal vortex energy gardens. These centers will be like a combination of a hospital and a school put together. The centers will provide health and well-being programs, rejuvenation chambers, color and sound crystal energy fields, integration training fields, and much more. They will be attunement centers, where all people can go and utilize on a regular basis, to keep their physical energy body operating in maximum balance as humanity expands and embodies more light frequency.

A wide array of services will be provided, as well as classes for education and training. The health and well-being of all people will always be one of the most important aspects of reality to provide greater harmonics of light for our kingdom of light's expansion. All souls will receive any and all energetic attunements necessary. There will be regular energy alignment profiles and programs that take place to maintain health, well-being, balance, and harmony for all.

This world will run as a whole unit. There will need to be sectors for proper alignment and overview of systems. They will run in the same manner. The elders of light will coordinate all activities of creation.

This will be a new type of world. In the beginning, we will all have to work together. This will be a must for survival, yes, but also now a natural way of being. All will realize this and work together.

The kingdom of light will not be complete until all
souls return home. All roads of creation eventually
converge; it is a mathematical energetic reality.

The one and the all. For one to complete our journey, we all
must. When the kingdom is completed another begins.

Our world of separateness is ending.

We have painted only a small picture of what the Future of
Creation will be like. Together as Unified Units of Light We Will
All Generate and Cocreate a Harmonious World that will be

a Masterpiece of Living Light.

Diamond Star

Chapter 7

Cocreation

All of us are our creator's children, sons and daughters of the creative force that has generated everything in existence. So you can say animate and inanimate. I say only animate. Everything has a life-force and is not stationary. All of creation is on the move. Everything in creation has a relationship with time and space.

There is a special quality within the human race, which is the fact that our creator planted the seed of creation in each and every one of us, the children of creation. The big difference is that we are creators also. Remember, I talked about time and our relationship with time. Well, all that training is now about to move to another level of reality. It is about to be expressed to us in a new and more fluid way. This, in turn, will open up our aperture of time and space to a greater degree, to be able to begin to take on a higher role in the creation of reality.

This new arena of time and space is this next cycle that is about to begin. This will be a new level of learning for all that will move into and onto this new aperture of light. Even the oldest of souls that are moving into this new sphere of influence have not had an embodiment such as this one that is coming. So one can say just like riding a bicycle? Well, if you have not ridden a bicycle for a few thousand years, and you are on a new type of bicycle, there is still a learning curve.

So yes, we will all be learning, living, expanding, and growing together. We will have to because we will each need each other. This will be the beginning and benchmark foundation of our future reality, supporting each other with unity, balance, and harmony. Supporting each other by working together. Everyone, no better, no less, only what is. Some with more age, and some with more light. I will tell you this, age does not necessarily denote light, but they do tend to hang out together.

So age and light. There is one big thing I wish to share here. Life is a journey. No beginning and no end. Only a constant flow of energy, the energy that was before it became us. Always there just the same. So I say again, no beginning and no end. I like to share with people, especially young people, we are all on our road of life. There is no destination. There is only the ride. So enjoy the ride. That is the trick to life. The present moment, the ride…

Taking time each moment on our ride of life. Expanding that moment of creative capacity. Stretching it in different directions in that moment of feeling it, as we begin to learn about this next level of time and space and our new level of cocreative relationship with it. All of our thoughts and feelings will be manifesting now at a much faster rate. Yes, very much so. We will all need to be very accountable for our thoughts and feelings because they will appear before us in the present moment for those with enough light.

The elders of light will take cocreation into a new parameter of reality. There will be timing and learning around these new energetic levels of light, color, and sound. All people everywhere will be in a process of cocreative expansion. Learning, creating, balancing, and harmonizing our energy of light, our energy of love. This will all be a natural and open field of growth and process of life for all. The idea of utilizing energy for power and control would be openly felt and known by all immediately. There also would be no system to be in power and control of, for there are no monetary systems or ownership of any kind.

All people will have the retention of what occurred in this last cycle and what is occurring right now on our planet. They will have no desire or feeling for any further ridiculous realities such as the one we live in currently. As we all develop our cocreative abilities, each soul of light will have a deep desire to fulfill its light presence and promise to our creator now that we have risen to a level of light to empower ourselves. Like a young person who gets the keys to their first automobile. A new big exciting responsibility, empowering us with a great sense of freedom. We will all be so busy rebuilding and aligning with these new frequencies, expanding, sharing new wonders, cocreating, living the fullness of life in a whole new way, in a beautiful new capacity with the rest of humanity in an ever-growing field of light.

The ride itself will be the adventure of lifetimes…

Every aspect of this entire world is going to completely change. How this world is run, how it is built, the type of food we eat, the way we learn and communicate, the need for military and weapons, everything is going to change.

Here is a list of some of the aspects of our life here on Mother Earth and what their changes will be like:

a. Energy
b. Food
c. Transportation
d. Waste
e. Soul Embodiment

Energy

Our new forms of energy for the planet and her people will all be completely clean and non-destructive on every level. Endless power for all. Completely free at our fingertips. Endless… With Earth's South Pole being activated, and higher fields of light coming to us now, all these electrical systems will step up to a new level of electron magnetics, beyond our current capacity of knowledge. The slightest little photoconductor attached to a microelectron capacitor could run a great deal of equipment for a long time with no heat or waste of any kind. It would be about the size of a book.

This is just one item. There will be so many new energy devices that are totally clean and nonpolluting. The biggest key to all these new machines are what I call energy assimilators. These can take on energetic magnetics from the source. Basically like a solar panel. Creation will not release these until we are well into this cycle. But this will allow humanity to expand the scope of its power systems greatly. Light assimilators are still the best bet because they have no moving parts and are totally clean and quiet.

New types of fusion will be brought forth for specialized space travel and our new Earth magnetic magnocars. No more roads or rubber tires to go flat. We will all simply cruise over the countryside. Oh, and all those power poles and wires that have been choking our mother? Well, they will not be there anymore, and we will not be putting them back.

There will be many new ways to utilize free energy. Depending on the area and application, this would be the main factor in choosing the appropriate system. Like I have been saying, only necessary energy applications will be utilized. First and foremost is the new outline and mandate of life with our mother. This mandate is one of love and respect. We, as our mother's children, will now hold our creative provider of physical form in very high regard with love and wish to honor that love by keeping this planet as natural as possible at all times.

Food

We all are what we eat. A very wonderful person I know has a saying, "Our food is our medicine." Made with love and eaten with gratitude. Remember, everything is energy, and energy responds to our thoughts and feelings of creation. Masaru Emoto photographed water and its crystalline structure when frozen. He showed how it responds to our energy and emotions. All positive emotions reflected beauty and harmony. All negative emotions reflected discord and imbalance. His work is a wonderful revelation of the energies of creation being represented physically in our lives, and also how much our thoughts and feelings affect all our realities of life. Humanity is at a new doorway of creation now as we all begin to cocreate with creation much more intrinsically. So love and bless your water, food, and everything in your life and have gratitude for it all to serve you, and it will.

As we all now begin to take on more light and utilize this new energy to a greater degree, we in turn shift our energy requirements. We begin to require lighter, less dense foods in our diet. As we each open to these new frequencies of light, we move from electro-magnetic and carbon-based fuels, which convert chemical into electrical energy, to an etheric-magnetic energy field and a new crystalline-based structure of reality. This operates in and with our light-body crystal energy field.

Our body structures now will require lighter and less dense higher vibrational energy food. Plant-based foods are photovoltaic energy foods and carry more light-field energies of color and sound in less dense carbon-based units, which in itself is shifting to a crystalline base also.

Our human bodies are shifting from carbon to crystalline structure at this time. This is the beginning of a new way of physical life and physical reality for the human being.

This has already begun to exist in our world. There are many new and exciting natural foods and ways to utilize them in our diet. Raw food is a key component because it retains the food's life-force energy. Energy is the key component here. Integrating our power of self is a constant endeavor on our stairway of light.

The more we each shift, the lighter our food requirements will become. It will be important now to keep our energy field and energy body fortified with less-dense energies of creation. Our new energy centers will provide easily accessible and easily utilized energy supplements for all to maintain their vibrational balance.

Eating very dense materials can take our energy bodies out of the moment, creating time and space for them independently or together. For instance, Thanksgiving, where everyone has to lie down after dinner. This has worked and was necessary in our past society of creation.

But this way of energy fortification is coming to an end. We will all now be opening to a new light energy field of reality, expressed in a higher dimension of physicality. All our nutritional and dietary programs will change drastically.

With this change in our light field, our diets will now be more momentary. All people everywhere will now hydrate and assimilate energy at more regular intervals. It will not be three squares a day any longer. This is what I meant when I said all homes will have a small kitchen. People will be utilizing energy in smaller quantities and more often. They will need to do this, especially in the beginning of this shift. This is why there will be energy stations for all to realign and balance their energy fields. A place to hydrate, have some energy food supplements, and relax in an energy portal of color and sound. Within ten to fifteen minutes of our time, a person would be refreshed and regenerated to full capacity to carry on. If not, they could stay as is necessary. All needs would always be met in direct response to desire and necessity with love and grace.

Our planet will become a beautiful garden of nature. Natural lands will be our new way of life and reality for Mother Earth, and for all. This world is meant to be raw and cutting edge in its scope, for humanity to expand its boundaries of creation's pure reality and essence of Life-Force. Our physical life and sustenance come from this reality.

This vibrance and its boldness of life are the thresholds of reality that define, refine, and reflect the human spirit of physical life.

Transportation

Come on down to Cycle Performance Center and pick up your new mag-mobile. They utilize microphoto electron cold fusion, modern-day George Jetson flying vehicles... Yes, definitely. Personal transportation, clean, clear, silent, and safe for our new reality. Only long-distance vehicles will be at high altitude. All local transportation will only need to be at a safe altitude to be unoffensive. Bicycle courses, walking paths? Yes. Roads? No.

Our new reality will be modern beyond belief. Yet set in an old movie scene on many levels of actual reality. While on one hand, we have the technology of advanced cultures, the new "in" will be old school, and oh boy, what a world to explore. Raw, new, and unexplored in many ways.

Our new Earth will be left open and whole. The old systems of power and communication lines along with roads of all kinds everywhere are finished. They will be taken off our mother and not replaced. They provided a burden of imbalance to her energy and physical body. They will not be replaced at all.

Our newly refreshed planet will only be traversed by air and water. Transportation centers will be set up around the globe for manufacturing, supply, storage, and delivery sites. We will still have local air shuttle services to different sites around the globe.

Once again, no machines of any kind will burn fuel any longer, such as the internal combustion engine or jet engine. This type of technology is invasive and destructive. There is a great deal of dark technology that is currently being utilized by the major governments of our world. While these technologies are very technically sound and represent great strides in advancement, they have very detrimental energy emissions to all life-forms on our planet.

There are many other new technologies that will perform well for humanity in this near future. Once again, since we are all working together now, there is a great deal of our cocreative effort that will no longer need to be generated since we will only be creating what we need as a whole. This fact alone will be a huge asset to humanity since we will only create what we need in the present moment.

Waste

Right here, right now: What is waste?

I see this all the time: one person's trash turns into another person's treasure. I bet if someone created a way to turn real trash into gold, it would disappear overnight, and the islands of trash in the middle of our oceans would become war zones. This is the mentality of our planet. This fact in itself is the epitome of waste and the reason we have waste. Our parameters of Creation have gotten so far out of balance that they interfere with our common sense, our values, even our basis of right and wrong. Once again, our personal judgments apply to everything, except our common sense and moral character. I have been sharing for quite some time that the smallest things in our world are the biggest… The tiniest, most unimportant part of your life says everything about you…

The United States has a huge role to play in this new world. Aside from being one of the new light centers for humanity (there are two), we have a huge role to play in reorganizing all we have disorganized. Yes, there will be a global reset of creation. Yes, many people will leave this planet but only to be reborn once again. The energy of what we all have generated in this world will now be brought into a new harmonic of balance as each soul endeavors to earn new levels of the light of our creator who will be watching our new footsteps. And what better way and better reason for us to apply our energy because even though we may have been misguided, the energies of whom we really are, and have really always been, are still there. We will all now live a clean, clear, loving role of life in our world.

Our new world will have no trash. All energies of creation will be organized from beginning to end. Everything will have a complete cycle of creation. First of all, in an organized society of whole people, there is no waste.

Only another Person's Treasure…

To live our lives in accordance with our creator's directive and love. Where there is no bottom line. Where there is nothing too small to care about. We all enter a new level of life and reality of consciousness, illumination, and creation itself.

Soul Embodiment

The seventh world of attunement...

Attunement: "To bring into harmony, make harmonious."

This is where we all become one of the Blues Brothers, a soul man, a time of soul empowerment and soul connection. In this cycle of creation, we all will be developing our relationship with our soul, now that we have generated a clear enough physical, emotional, and mental structure of embodiment. Now our core soul energy body will be able to develop a real relationship with its physical aspect of form. This will move all people onto the next level of their empowerment, at the soul level of creation.

Our New Cycle of Adventure...

This cycle begins with all who have achieved this level of advancement at its base level of creation to begin our journey of real empowerment and partnership with our higher aspiration of self, our soul. This reality of creation is coming forward now, sensitizing the human body to evolve into a relationship with its soul light body of creation. This now opens a new door.

In this cycle and previous cycles, all people spent time developing their energy body in relation to the self. This evolution of life occurred throughout eons of time and space, each of us working with our energy bodies, developing a relationship with these bodies physically, mentally, emotionally, and spiritually.

All creation is wanting to get in line with this ride. But I can tell you, it is a long line, and there are a lot of requirements to move to this reality of life and light. There have been many preparations made throughout time and space for this period of time arriving now.

We, as in everyone on this planet, in this new arena of time and space about to occur, will be in for the ride of creation. On this very special ride, we will all be blessed with new opportunities to expand our energy light fields of creation. Our souls will have a closer connection with us, their aspects of form. Our little voice will now become our best friend.

As our core essence energy soul light field of creation comes forward now to begin its embodiment with us, we each begin a new level of creative form. This will be a very fulfilling adventure of time and space in creation.

This is all new. This is very big and intense energetically for our souls to come to us and begin to unite with each of us in our own way. To open up to allow us new levels of creative empowerment. As our creator steps forward now expanding our energies of creation and our soul body comes to us to empower us with its love and grace, our world has just changed.

Mother Earth herself will also now step up in octaves of color and sound. We all will have a great deal more love, light, wisdom, and grace to shine and to share.

I Am—I Know—It Is

This Beautiful New World will become Heaven on Earth.
Light never stops its journey. Our light
field energy will Expand Forever.

"To be or not to be?"—that is our only question.

The symphonies of light from the soul level of creation will play
for us, empower us, and become one with us, as long as we each
can adhere to the mandates of life and of Creations Universal Law.

All in the Key of Life…

Along with the Angels; Faith, Hope, Love and Grace on Our
Journey Through-Out the Time and Space of Creation.

Journey Well, My Friends!

Epilogue

The Cycles of Creation

This is book 2 of *The Cycles of Creation* book series. There are sixteen books in the series altogether. Each of the books in this series has been written to assist each reader on their path, their journey, of life. *The Cycle* series of books are all Energy Guides that will outline the changes that are coming for Creation over this next Light Cycle and beyond. The changes that they outline are vast, wondrous, and wonderful. We are as young children now on an eternal voyage of life that will evolve infinitely. Whether you believe them or not, these books are an exciting adventure through time and space that will expand each reader's consciousness, reality, and horizon of life.

I ask everyone to open your minds and your hearts to receive the truths that they hold for you. No two artists will ever paint the same picture. So my advice is not to try. Everything in creation is an original.

Be original.

May these books guide you on your journey of Light with Love.

C

The Cycles of Creation Books

1. The Presence
2. Aquarius
3. Genesis
4. The Key of Life
5. The Golden Age
6. The New Atlantis
7. The Inner Kingdom
8. The Sacred Journey
9. The Light Codes of Creation
10. The Crystalline Realm
11. The Light Spheres of Creation
12. The Tonal Doorway
13. Perfected Perfection
14. The Interstellar Alliance
15. Christ's Golden Age
16. The Longest Journey

Clifford Kenneth Platt III
cliffordkennethplatt111@gmail.com

For a great period of this incarnation, I have been Clif LaPlant. As I grow, I am finding that I cannot escape the reality of who I really am and must now openly face and embrace it instead. To now accept and own the truth and empowerment that my Soul and Creation are revealing to me and to us all. This is a New Reality for All Humanity now to take on.

This book is not about me; it is an energetic profile for us all to open our minds and hearts so we may each receive our next level of Soul Existence of form on and with Mother Earth and beyond. The Energy of Creation from our Soul level is here now for those that are ready and willing. This book is a profile of this new reality coming to us all now, and how we can each embrace it, and empower ourselves with it, from within.

Love and Blessings on Your Journey!

Printed in the USA
CPSIA information can be obtained
at www.ICGtesting.com
CBHW040546190824
13304CB00066BA/1489